T0005876

Acting
in the Wake

Acting in the Wake

Prayers for Justice

COLLECTED PRAYERS OF
WALTER BRUEGGEMANN, VOLUME 1

WALTER BRUEGGEMANN

WITH BARBARA DICK

WJK WESTMINSTER
JOHN KNOX PRESS
LOUISVILLE • KENTUCKY

First edition
Published by Westminster John Knox Press
Louisville, Kentucky

23 24 25 26 27 28 29 30 31 32 — 10 9 8 7 6 5 4 3 2 1

Book design by Drew Stevens
Cover design by Mary Ann Smith

Library of Congress Cataloging-in-Publication Data

Names: Brueggemann, Walter, author.
Title: Acting in the wake : prayers for justice : collected prayers of
  Walter Brueggemann / Walter Brueggemann, with Barbara Dick.
Description: First edition. | Louisville, Kentucky : Westminster John Knox
  Press, [2023] | Summary: "This collection of prayers for use in both
  public worship and private devotion run the gamut from particular days
  in the church year to special moments in the lives of worshiping
  communities to events playing out on the world stage, spurring us toward
  acts of justice and peacemaking and calling on God to heal and restore
  God's hurting and broken people"-- Provided by publisher.
Identifiers: LCCN 2022047644 (print) | LCCN 2022047645 (ebook) | ISBN
  9780664266165 (paperback) | ISBN 9781646982998 (ebook)
Subjects: LCSH: Prayers for justice.
Classification: LCC BV245 .B676 2023 (print) | LCC BV245 (ebook) | DDC
  242/.8--dc23/eng/20221125
LC record available at https://lccn.loc.gov/2022047644
LC ebook record available at https://lccn.loc.gov/2022047645

CONTENTS

ONE: PRAYERS OF *WE* JUSTICE

TWO: PRAYERS OF *THOU* JUSTICE

In his teaching, preaching, writing, and praying, Walter Brueggemann testifies to a deep and abiding relationship with both the biblical text and the astonishing God who abides in and cannot be disentangled from that text. Both seem to grasp him without ever quite being grasped by him.

He puts on the biblical text like a well-worn, coarse-wool coat. It's no comfy barn jacket, nor a glorious coat of many colors. It's a garment that never quite fits: it pinches, scratches, bunches, and binds; it's a little too warm in the summer and not warm enough in the winter; and it's never really in style. Yet there's no imagining him going out without it. Brueggemann understands that this peculiar text lives and moves and has its being in our own peculiar lives, individual and corporate, as we grapple with it and try to put it on. He reminds us that one must keep one hand on the page, with all its odd particularity, and the other on one's own oddly particular passion, pathos, and pain.

There is nothing like sitting around a seminar table and a biblical text with him. He always puts his whole self into his engagements with the text and with his students, and he expects no less from them. Still, as exciting as it is to be in the front row at one of his lectures, ducking flying chalk fragments and dodging a right jab as he reenacts Moses parting the Red Sea, what is most remarkable is his love for this fascinating and often disturbingly strange text that we call Bible. He helps us understand that biblical theology, like all good theology, is at its best poetry, a bold and subversive act of creative world-making, inviting us to imagine bold alternatives to the prose-flattened script of commodification and violence that the empire wants us to believe is the only realistic possibility. In so doing he shows us what he means when he writes, in his *Theology of the Old Testament*, that "the interpreter must be an at-risk participant in a rhetorical process in which being is regularly at stake in and through utterance."

Nowhere is this risky imaginative participation in alternative world-making more in evidence than in his public prayers. Indeed, I still remember many of the prayers he offered at the beginnings of seminar meetings when I was his student in the late 1980s and early '90s. There were never any polite formalities of opening and closing; he would simply walk into the room, drop his stack of books and notes on the seminar table, and start talking. I don't recall him bowing his head or folding his hands or closing his eyes. He just started in, without warning. Sometimes it took the rest of us in the room a second to realize that he, indeed we, were now in prayer. One especially memorable prayer went something like this:

> We walk through minefields
> wondering where you might show up
> to rescue or undo us.

I believe that was it, the whole thing. No "Let us pray," no "Dear God" to start, no exposition or explication of the terse words, no "Amen" to finish. Only this densely concentrated, profoundly fraught utterance from "we" to "you." We walk. You show up, rescue, undo.

Then as now, his prayers always began with either "we" or "you." The one to whom the prayer was addressed was not some third-person God that we already know *about* from inherited doctrines and confessions. Allied with Martin Buber's understanding of the "I-thou" relationship between oneself and another, as opposed to an "I-it" dynamic of separation and objectification, these prayers invoked a "we-you" relationship in which each party is vulnerable to and impinged upon by the other in ways that cannot be objectified or reduced to formulae.

I don't recall him ever typing or writing out his prayers back then. Nor does he. Thankfully, he did write them out for other public occasions, and eventually he started doing so for his classes. And so we have the remarkable gift of this book. Along with his earlier collections, the prayers gathered here carry that distinctive at-risk theological generativity that we so need in these times. They are boldly experimental, creatively and provocatively drawing from the biblical pool of imagination in order to conjure new social and theological possibilities on new horizons of meaning. Akin to his understanding of the prophetic imagination as poetic and world-creative, his prayers are often stunningly affronting, echoing biblical rhetorical patterns and images even as they interrupt and subvert them. He experiments with language in ways that break onto startling images of and agonistic engagements with God.

Echoing Buber's *I and Thou*, another title for this book could have been *We and Thou*. As Brueggemann writes, its division into "Prayers of *We* Justice" and "Prayers of *Thou* Justice" aims to make clear that justice work is a "bilateral, covenantal enterprise" between the work "we" do and the work "you" do. "The *we-prayers*," he writes, "bespeak a resolve to engage in the troublesome, glorious work of justice as our proper human preoccupation. This work of justice requires of human agents courage, stamina, energy, and durability, because it is labor against greatly entrenched powers that are in part propelled by demonic resolve."

Still, the title he has given us is *Acting in the Wake*. What to make of that? In the wake of what? In the wake of catastrophic sufferings and injustices, to be sure: there are prayers from the near wake of the attacks of September 11, 2001, and other terrors; and prayers in the wake of devastating political moments; and prayers in the midst and wake of war. As he reminds us in other writings, all these wakes are aftermaths of our delusional claims to chosenness and exceptionalism, and they call for forms of prayer that can help us break through such delusions toward paradoxically humbler yet bolder action.

But there is another potential meaning of "acting in the wake," one that comes from the prayer that bears the same title: acting in the wake of "you," our "gospel God."

We live and move in your wake.
and so after you;
we practice your habits of justice,
　　　　　　your well-being,
　　　　　　your safety,
　　　　　　your mercy and your compassion,
　　　　　　your faithfulness.

Acting in the wake: living and moving and having our being in your wake, following after and drawing close to your best, most just ways of being in this world. And therefore acting, and praying, in the wake of Jesus, who "has broken the force of violence" so that we are free to act and speak differently, with one another and with you, *Thou* Justice.

Timothy Beal

⎯⎯⎯⎯⎯ ∽◯∽ ⎯⎯⎯⎯⎯

From early on, the Christian tradition has under-stood prayer to be "a conversation with God." Already in the fourth century, John Chrysostom took prayer as "continual conversation with God that proceeds from longing for God."[1] His contem-porary, Augustine, added, "Prayer is the conversa-tion of the heart addressed to God." I learned that formulation from the catechism in this way:

> Prayer is the conversation of the heart with God for the purpose of praising him, asking him to supply the needs of ourselves and others, and thanking him for whatever he gives us.[2]

My father, August, my pastor and confirmation teacher, shortened it for us thirteen-year-olds:

> Prayer is the conversation of the heart addressed to God.

Since prayer is conversation with God, it is cru-cial at the outset to identify this God. This is not "the unmoved mover" of Greek philosophy. Nor is this the "ground of being" of more contemporary philosophy. Rather, the God who is party to this conversation is the one traced out graphically and dramatically in the memory of ancient Israel. This is the one who is pledged in loyalty to benefit God's people and to the well-being of creation, and who is known to exercise a full range of emotional capacity. This God can be attested only in imagery and rhetoric that is personal and interpersonal, so that God can be impinged upon, is capable of response, and can readily be the subject of active effective verbs. Unless and until God is trusted and voiced in the dialect of Israel's memory, it is likely that we will not have entered into the dramatic depth and saving helpfulness of biblical prayer.

At the outset, this means that such practice of prayer resists the popular familiar renderings of God as "omnipotent, omnipresent, and omniscient," in order to embrace covenantal, relational categories that are, for example, on full exhibit in the poetic construal of Hosea:

> I will take you for my wife in *righteousness* and in *justice*, in *steadfast love*, and in *mercy*. I will take you for my wife in *faithfulness*; and you shall know the LORD. (Hos. 2:19–20, emphasis added)

These five terms set forth the profoundly interpersonal casting of this God to whom we may pray.

This shift from the safe philosophical categories to the risky exposé of covenant engagement is difficult for many people who have been socialized and nurtured into the reasoned terms of modernity. That reasoned way of articulating God tempts us variously to self-sufficiency because God cannot and does not engage, or to timidity because God cannot be moved by our best passion, or to despair because we are on our own. But prayer cast in the covenantal categories of a biblical life-world has no need to settle for self-sufficiency, timidity, or despair.

The notion of prayer as conversation is rooted for Christians in the Old Testament practice of prayer that is variously rendered in the book of Psalms, the book of Lamentations, and the traditions of Moses and Jeremiah.[3] Thus Moses could remonstrate with God and engage in back-and-forth, face-to-face exchange:

> O LORD, why does your wrath burn hot against your people, whom you brought out of the land of Egypt with great power and with a mighty hand? Why should the Egyptians say, "It was with evil intent that he brought them out to kill them in the mountains, and to consume them from the face of the earth"? Turn from your fierce wrath; change your mind and do not bring disaster on your people. Remember Abraham, Isaac, and Israel, your servants, how you swore to them by your own self, saying to them, "I will multiply your descendants like the stars of heaven, and all this land that I have promised I will give to your descendants, and they shall inherit it forever." (Exod. 32:11–13; see vv. 14–17)

In the depth of Israel's crisis, Moses' prayer is simply asking:

> If now I have found favor in your sight, O Lord, I pray, let the Lord go with us. Although

this is a stiff-necked people, pardon our iniquity and our sin, and take us for your inheritance.
(34:9–10)

In each of these cases, Moses' prayer caused God
to act afresh.

Jeremiah's prayers closely echo the laments of
the book of Psalms that variously voice *complaint*,
petition, and *doxology*:

Why is my pain unceasing,
  my wound incurable,
    refusing to be healed?
Truly, you are to me like a deceitful brook,
  like waters that fail.

Jer. 15:18

Heal me, O LORD, and I shall be healed;
  save me, and I shall be saved;
    for you are my praise.

17:14

Sing to the LORD;
  praise the LORD!
For he has delivered the life of the needy
  from the hands of evildoers.

20:13

Karl Barth looms large in any effort to articu-
late a Reformed, evangelical notion of prayer. His
remarkable discussion of prayer, so instructive
for me, sets prayer alongside faith and obedience,
so that the triad of "faith, obedience, and prayer"
must all be taken together.[4] While Barth's thought
is complex enough, I single out three claims that

have been focal for my own thought and my own prayer.

First, Barth asserts that prayer is "simply asking."[5] Barth of course acknowledges other dimensions of prayer, but sees petition as the core act:

> Asking is the only thing that he can do, the only spontaneous response that he can make. When he asks for it, when he says to God: I have not, and Thou hast; Therefore give me what Thou hast and I have not, he acknowledges and magnifies God Himself as Giver, and he honours the divine nature of that which he is able to take and receive.[6]

Barth dares to identify the church as "the asking community":

> Thus the asking community stands together with its Lord before God on behalf of all creation. . . . The asking of this community anticipates as it were that of creation as a whole. It gives voice and expression to the groaning of creation.[7]

Second, Barth recognizes that prayer impinges upon God and changes God:

> God is not deaf, but listens; more than that, he acts. God does not act in the same way whether we pray or not. Prayer exerts an influence on God's action, even upon his existence. This is what the word "answer" means.[8]

Thus, in The Heidelberg Catechism that Barth cites:

> For my prayer is much more certainly heard by
> God than I am persuaded in my heart that I de-
> sire such things from him.[9]

This of course is the crucial point of prayer. The statement that our prayer can effectively impinge upon God is a deep embarrassment to any modern person. That is why we get the familiar cant that "prayer changes the one who prays" or "families that pray together stay together." Such instrumental value may be correct, but it is beside the point. To be sure, God answers our prayers in freedom; that, however, does not tell against the God who answers. This point requires, for many people, a radical revision of our sense about who God is. And, *mutatis mutandis*, it requires an alternate sense of self and a fresh sense of the we who constitute the "asking community."[10]

Third (what I suppose I have gotten from Barth via Jacques Ellul) is that we pray because we are commanded to pray. This is not the command of a fearful tyrant. It is rather the command of our caring father to whom we turn when we "come to ourselves," of our engaged mother who does not forget compassion for the children of her womb (see Isa. 49:14–15). It belongs to us as beloved children of God to pray. Such prayer is constitutive of our being because our being is as trusting children who may ask, seek, and knock in order to receive what we need for our lives. Thus, for Barth, an evangelical discernment of prayer requires a practice of faith and obedience that is completely at odds with the practice of most conventional piety and spirituality.

A second, more accessible instruction in prayer is *Help, Thanks, Wow* by Anne Lamott.[11] While I did not learn these basics from her, Lamott's book has well chronicled for me a helpful taxonomy for prayer. Her book title suggests three moments that are characteristic of prayer.

First, *Help!* The acknowledgment of dependence in the form of petition echoes Barth's "simply asking." For persons who have "come of age" on modernity, such asking for help seems superfluous. Except, of course, that we arrive, soon or late, at a failure of self-sufficiency, if nowhere else, then as we are confronted with the threat of death. But, of course, the threat of death comes in many forms and different degrees all day long. Indeed, one may conclude that the normative narrative of the Bible begins with Hebrew slaves exactly at that moment of an urgent cry for help amid the deathly demands of Pharaoh:

> The Israelites groaned under their slavery, and cried out. (Exod. 2:23)

It may be (as with these slaves) that the petition for help is, in the first instance, not even addressed to anyone. As that text has it, however, the emancipatory God of the exodus is like a magnet that draws such desperate petition to God's self even if not addressed to that God: "Their cry for help rose up to God." Or, as Isaiah wondrously has it later:

> Before they call I will answer,
>   while they are yet speaking I will hear.
> *Isa. 65:24*

Second for Lamott is *Thanks.* God's generous attentiveness evokes gratitude that becomes the mainspring of a life of joyous obedience. Thanks, of course, is the glad awareness that we are not, cannot be, and need not be self-sufficient. Thus, gratitude pervades a life of faith:

> Pray without ceasing, give thanks in all circumstances; for this is the will of God in Christ Jesus for you. (1 Thess. 5:17–18)

Paul, moreover, sees that thanks provides a framework for petition and identifies the practice of thanks to God as a forceful antidote to worry:

> Do not worry about anything, but in everything by prayer and supplication with thanksgiving let your requests be made known to God. (Phil. 4:6)

In this bottomless gratitude, Paul recognizes that everything we have is a gift that we did not produce or possess:

> What do you have that you did not receive? And if you received it, why do you boast as if it were not a gift? (1 Cor. 4:7)

Third for Lamott is *Wow!* A biblical rendering of wow is the practice of praise, the eager, glad, unrestrained ceding of self over to God and God's goodness. Such a wow is an embarrassment for the self-sufficient because we are swept away in awe before the one who is the source of our life. Rather than the cheap glib *awesome* of popular culture, the act of wow-praise goes to the depth of our existence. Such a wow is beyond the specificity and inventory of thanks wherein we "count our blessings." Praise holds nothing back in calculation concerning the God-givenness of our lives in daily proportion. Such *wow* may be as brief as Israel's shortest psalm:

> Praise the LORD, all you nations!
>> Extol him, all you peoples!
> For great is his steadfast love toward us,
>> and the faithfulness of the LORD endures forever.
> Praise the LORD!

Ps. 117

That psalm lacks the specificity that we may bring as we sing; it invites focus on the utter reliability (*'emeth*) and tenacious solidarity (*hesed*) of God toward us. Or we may sing wow with the utter self-abandonment of Psalm 150:

> Praise him with trumpet sound;
>> praise him with lute and harp!
> Praise him with tambourine and dance;
>> praise him with strings and pipe!
> Praise him with clanging cymbals;
>> praise him with loud clashing cymbals!
> Let everything that breathes praise the LORD!
> Praise the LORD!

vv. 3–6

Such a *wow* has no need for specificity because the wonder is all the way from the self over to God who defies all our best explanatory reasoning.[12] Given the modern "turn to the subject," wow-praise is a subversive activity because it is an eager, passionate "turn away from the subject" back to the Thou who makes the self possible.

Lamott's triad is hugely instructive. I suggest, however, that a fourth capacity belongs indispensably to faithful prayer: *Rats!* The faithful know that, many times, things do not work out, the center does not hold, and death crowds us. Such lived reality may be voiced in honest prayer to God concerning a variety of adversaries. The faithful, replicating ancient Israel, keep before God something of an "enemies list," the names of those whom we may wish ill:

> May his children be orphans,
>   and his wife a widow.
> May his children wander about and beg;
>   may they be driven out of the ruins they inhabit.
> May the creditor seize all that he has,
>   may strangers plunder the fruits of his toil.
> May there be no one to do him a kindness,
>   nor anyone to pity his orphaned children.
> May his posterity be cut off;
>   may his name be blotted out in the second
>   generation.
>
> *Ps. 109:9–13*

Of course, Jesus taught us to love our enemies. But before that is possible, we must tell the truth about our enemies to God, all of the truth, including our worst hope for them.

In our faithful prayer, moreover, we do not hesitate to call God to account. God is not an automatic answering machine; God works in freedom. Those who pray faithfully need not hesitate to call God to account and so summon God to faithful action when God is seen to be remiss:

> Rouse yourself! Why do you sleep, O Lord?
>> Awake, do not cast us off forever!
> . . . .
> Rise up, come to our help.
>> Redeem us for the sake of your steadfast love.
>>> *Ps. 44:23, 26*

> Every day I call on you, O LORD;
>> I spread out my hands to you.
> . . . .
> But I, O LORD, cry out to you,
>> in the morning my prayer comes before you.
>>> *Ps. 88:9, 13*

It may, of course, be judged that such prayer is *pre-Christian* or *unchristian*. That, however, is not the case because the church always has before it the psalms of lament, complaint, and protest from the Old Testament. We need only consider that Jesus is remembered for his accusation of infidelity from God on the cross:

> And about three o'clock Jesus cried with a loud voice, "Eli, Eli, lema sabachthani?" that is, "My God, my God, why have you forsaken me?" (Matt. 27:46; Mark 15:34; see Ps. 22:1)

It is that reality of deep abandonment that scars the life of both Father and Son. Jürgen Moltmann has it forcefully:

> The Fatherlessness of the Son is matched by the Sonlessness of the Father, and if God has constituted self as the Father of Jesus Christ, then he also suffers the death of his Fatherhood in the death of the Son.[13]

It is the prayer of the forsaken! The faithful who pray have always known and trusted that the God addressed is the one "from whom no secret can be hid." We need not hide that dark side of our consternation; we may properly voice it in our conversation of the heart addressed to God. When we consider the regime of *help/thanks/wow/rats*, we have before us the full spectrum of human reality, all of which is offered to God in honest trust.

The practice of leading public prayer (as in the prayers in this collection) is an act of inviting and engaging the present company in that conversation of the heart. As a result, the voicing of prayer needs to be specific enough to have content, but porous enough not to coerce, permitting others present to bring their own nuance to that conversation of the heart. I suggest two exercises of prayer that may aid in this invitation and engagement. First, I have found it helpful to pray Scripture back to God. In my case, as a teacher of biblical texts, I have found it useful to appeal to the text under study as a guide to structure a prayer for the day. The most dramatic instance of which I know of praying Scripture back to God is the exemplar of Exodus 34:6–7 being employed by Moses in Numbers 14:18. In the Exodus passage, God's self-disclosure to Moses goes like this:

The LORD, the LORD,
a God merciful and gracious,
slow to anger,
and abounding in steadfast love and faithfulness,
keeping steadfast love for the thousandth generation,
forgiving iniquity and transgression and sin,
yet by no means clearing the guilty,
but visiting the iniquity of the parents
upon the children
and the children's children,
to the third and the fourth generation.

In a subsequent crisis in the wilderness, Israel has experienced God's neglect and indifference, which places Israel in peril. Moses prays to God in a way that calls God to account and reminds God of God's own self-disclosure, as though God has forgotten God's own commitments:

Then the Egyptians will hear of it, for in your might you brought up this people from among them, and they will tell the inhabitants of this land. They have heard that you, O LORD, are in the midst of this people; for you, O LORD, are seen face to face, and your cloud stands over them and you go in front of them, in a pillar of cloud by day and in a pillar of fire by night. Now if you kill this people all at one time, then the nations who have heard about you will say, "It is because the LORD was not able to bring this people into the land he swore to give them that he has slaughtered them in the wilderness." And now, therefore, let the power of the LORD be great in the way that you promised when you spoke, saying,

> "The LORD is slow to anger,
> and abounding in steadfast love,
> forgiving iniquity and transgression,
> but by no means clearing the guilty,
> visiting the iniquity of the parents
> upon the children
> to the third and the fourth generation."

> Forgive the iniquity of this people according to the greatness of your steadfast love, just as you have pardoned this people, from Egypt even until now. (Num. 14:13–19)

The core act of Moses is to reiterate in verse 18 the very words of God in order to remind God of who God is and what God has promised. The appeal is followed in verse 19 by an imperative petition from Moses grounded in verse 18: "Forgive the iniquity of this people according to your steadfast love" (so clearly declared back in Exod. 34).

In verse 20, it is reported that God responds to the imperative of Moses. I have found that very many texts serve well for such a "pray back."

Second, prayer that engages the assembled community in the conversation with specificity and porousness requires an act of playful imagination so that we may move beyond the familiar and predictable clichés with daring suggestiveness. Such imaginative playfulness invites attentiveness to image and metaphor, and a turn of phrase that might be joltingly honest, risky, or even contrary. Thus, the conversation aims not simply to repeat the familiar but to engage both parties to the prayer (God and the assembly) in a fresh discernment of the issue at hand to which response may be made.

The prayers in this collection have arisen in actual practice in many local congregations and in many seminary classrooms. They are, to some extent, time and context specific, though I judge they may be useful resources for our ongoing practice of public prayer.

This collection, consisting of many of my public prayers, has had a meandering development. The blessed Ed Searcy worked long over them. The beloved Joe Phelps did attentive work on them as well. And the blessed, well-beloved Tia Brueggemann saw to its completion. I am grateful as well to David Dobson and the staff at Westminster John Knox Press (as I always am!) for willingness to publish the collection. I am grateful to my treasured colleague, Timothy Beal, for writing a generous foreword. And I am grateful to the host of the faithful who have prayed these prayers along with me. Prayer allows us to enter into blessed companionship. At the same time, it is also our ultimate defense against the seductions of self-sufficiency, timidity, and despair, and a means of resistance against instrumental reasoning and commoditization, against the force of Death that surveils us relentlessly and aggressively. The catechism can make for us a final affirmation, albeit in a patriarchal dialect:

> Our heavenly Father desires us and all his children to call upon him with cheerful confidence, as beloved children entreat a kind and affectionate father, knowing that he is both willing and able to help us.[14]

Notes

1. John Chrysostom, "Homily 6 on Prayer."

2. *Evangelical Catechism* (St. Louis: Eden Publishing House, 1929), 59.

3. See esp. Kathleen O'Connor, *Lamentations and the Tears of the World* (Maryknoll, NY: Orbis Books, 2002).

4. Karl Barth, *Church Dogmatics*, III/3, *The Doctrine of Creation* (Edinburgh: T. & T. Clark, 1961), 265–88.

5. Barth, *Church Dogmatics*, 268.

6. Barth, *Church Dogmatics*, 274.

7. Barth, *Church Dogmatics*, 279.

8. Karl Barth, *Prayer: 50th Anniversary Edition* (Louisville, KY: Westminster John Knox Press, 2002), 13.

9. *The Heidelberg Catechism: 400th Anniversary Edition 1563–1963* (Philadelphia: United Church Press, 1962), 126.

10. On the we of the asking community, see Franz Rosenzweig, *The Star of Redemption* (Notre Dame, IN: University of Notre Dame Press, 1985), 236, 325, and passim.

11. Anne Lamott, *Help, Thanks, Wow: The Three Essential Prayers* (New York: Penguin Books, 2012).

12. On wonder as the depth of faithful engagement, see William P. Brown, *Wisdom's Wonder: Character, Creation, and Crisis in the Bible's Wisdom Literature* (Grand Rapids: Eerdmans, 2014); Abraham Heschel, *I Asked for Wonder: A Spiritual Anthology*, ed. Samuel H. Dresner (New York: Crossroad, 1987).

13. Jürgen Moltmann, *The Crucified God: The Cross of Christ as the Foundation and Criticism of Christian Theology* (New York: Harper & Row, 1974), 243.

14. *Evangelical Catechism*, 60.

The God of the gospel has always cared in urgent ways about restorative socioeconomic and political justice. In our time, however, it has required the stirrings of liberation theology to teach us again about the centrality of justice for gospel faith. These stirrings have included the great initiatives of the Latin American church, and in more recent times the quest for justice for Black people (lately Black Lives Matter), for women (lately the MeToo movement), and the cause of LGBTQ+ persons. Under the tutelage of such movements we have learned afresh that justice for the left behind, excluded, and disempowered requires reallocation of societal resources and redistribution of political power. Thus justice entails disruption of business as usual in the body politic, a disruption that predictably disturbs those of us who have been privileged and advantaged by current arrangements.

The *We-Thou* juxtaposition of these prayers indicates that the work of justice is a bilateral, covenantal enterprise that involves both human work and the work of the gospel God. The *we-prayers* bespeak a resolve to engage in the troublesome, glorious work of justice as our proper human preoccupation. This work of justice requires of human agents courage, stamina, energy, and durability, because it is labor against greatly entrenched powers that are in part propelled by demonic resolve.

At the same time, we know that justice cannot be simply a human enterprise, because it is labor against "principalities and powers"; its eager exercise requires the resolve and engagement of the holy God (see Eph. 6:12). Thus *robust resolve* on our part for justice is matched by *robust confidence* in the authority and capacity of the holy God to whom we pray. The God to whom we pray for justice is no "nice God" who readily fits into our preferred comfort zones. Rather, this God is an active agent who works God's own holy purpose for the full restoration of creation in all its fruitful splendor. It is the work of our *Thou-prayers* to urge, move, and mobilize God to actions that authorize and cohere with our own faithful actions for justice.

Those who pray the *we-prayers* are often, like me, beneficiaries of great privilege. Thus the prayers are in fact a bold contradiction of our seeming best interest. We pray such prayers, nevertheless, because we have come to understand that our "seeming best interest" is less than the health of the community (and the world) of which we are an inescapable part. Those who pray the *Thou-prayers* are those who have moved beyond our comfortable bourgeois religion to grasp in some serious way the radicality of the gospel. Indeed, whenever we pray, we address the God who, via Moses, has declared, "Justice, and only justice, you shall pursue" (Deut. 16:20). That verdict via Moses, moreover, is echoed and reiterated by Jesus in his warning to the religious establishment of his day:

> Woe to you, scribes and Pharisees, hypocrites! For you tithe mint, dill, and cummin, and have neglected the weightier matters of the [Torah]: justice and mercy and faith. (Matt. 23:23)

Thus these prayers—the *we-prayers* of resolve and the *Thou-prayers* of petition—are words and actions that have confidence in the coming governance of God. In a deep way, all of our faithful prayers are echoes of the church's great prayer for justice in which we bid that God's kingdom will be "on earth as it is in heaven." The Lord's Prayer is an act of defiant hope and expectation. All of our other faithful prayers are articulations of that same hope. When the church prays that prayer and its other prayers, it acknowledges the "kingdom, power, and glory" belong only to the Lord of creation, and to none of the pretenders who stalk the earth. In the end, all of our prayers for justice are variations on "Come, Lord Jesus" (Rev. 22:20). This petition is not some imaginary dispensationalism. It is rather the conviction that God's rule shows up here and there, sometimes hidden, sometimes dramatic. Whenever and wherever Jesus comes in his rule, justice is on its way. This is justice that permits heaven and earth to sing as creation comes to its full wondrous performance:

> Say among the nations, "The LORD is king!
>   The world is firmly established; it shall never be moved.

He will judge the peoples with equity."
Let the heavens be glad, and let the earth rejoice;
    let the sea roar, all that fills it;
    let the field exult, and everything in it.
Then shall all the trees of the forest sing for joy
    before the LORD; for he is coming,
    for he is coming to judge the earth.
He will judge the world with righteousness,
    and the peoples with his truth.

Ps. 96:10–13

Every time we join in *we-prayers* and *Thou-prayers*, we join this great anthem of expectation.

Walter Brueggemann
Columbia Theological Seminary

ONE

PRAYERS OF *WE* JUSTICE

We are a strange mix of
   amber waves of grain
      and
   rockets' red glare.
We are a people blessed with flourishing land that
is marked by beauty and prosperity. We are, at the
same time, a people bent on war and domination,
violence, and torture. We mumble about our ambi-
guity. And then we notice that we are in free fall:
      We have messed up the amber waves of grain
         with our fossil fuel economy;
      We have settled for brutalizing metaphors
         for our national strength and pride.
      And so many—more and more—are left behind.
And now today, amid loud rhetoric,
defiant stalemate, and cynical exclusion toned with
racism,
   We pause.
We pause in your presence,
   For a moment of candor,
   For an instant of yielding,
   For a prospect of receiving from you.
What we hope for in this pause of prayer is that
   You will attend to us in our anxiety;
   You will forgive us in our small-mindedness;
   You will engage us for your work of justice;
   You will restore us to the sanity of neighborliness;
   You will work your will for peace and shalom
      among us,

Through us,
In spite of us,
Beyond us.
We are a conundrum of competing
        loyalties and ideologies.
So call us beyond ourselves,
        That shared amber waves of grain
            will prevail
        Over fearful red rockets that glare.
We pray in the name of Jesus who wept over Jerusalem
        and who lingers amid our shambled cities.
            Amen.

—May 1, 2014, Columbia Theological Seminary

We know well the "honor roll" of nation-states and mighty empires that run all the way from Egypt and Assyria to Britain and Japan and Russia and finally us. We know about the capacity for order that they have, and the accompanying capacity for exploitation and violence. We know that the great powers, while held in your hand, are tempted to autonomy and arrogance.

In the midst of war and in the wake of the election, we ponder modern empire and our tacit complicity in the current venture. In these moments, we hold our own resource-devouring empire up in your presence. For the moment, we pray for it . . .
forgiveness for its violence,
authority for its vision of freedom,
chastening for its distorted notion of peace.

We pray, for the moment, that our very own empire may be a vehicle for your good purposes. Beyond that, we pray the old hope of our faith:
That the kingdoms of this world
would become the kingdom of our God
and of his Christ.

We do not doubt that you will reign forever and ever. Along with all waiting powers, we sing gladly,
Forever and ever,
Hallelujah!
Hallelujah! Amen.

—November 4, 2004, Columbia Theological Seminary

We pray, as often as we can,
   "Your kingdom come on earth."
But our version of your rule is all mixed
   up with our interests and passions and
   cheaper commitments.

We pray, as often as we can,
   "Your will be done
     on earth as it is in heaven."
But our take on your will is all entwined
   with our frightened conservative ideologies
     or
   our shrill liberal passions.

And when we pray for your kingdom and your will,
   we ask for far more than we intended to ask . . .
     but we do know better.
   We do know that your kingdom
     is one of weakness amid our
        many strengths,
     is one of foolishness amid
        our deep wisdom,
     is one of poverty amid our
        cherished wealth.

We do know better . . .
   and so, in a moment of pause
   we pray that your
     kingdom will overrule the rulers of this age.

We pray that your will
    will subvert our will.
That we will be drawn toward your
    kingdom and your will,
    that we may depart to new justice
            and new peace and
            new joy.

We pray in the weak, poor, foolish
            name of Jesus. Amen.

—October 10, 2006

(Beginning a Class on Psalms)

The realities are as fresh as yesterday,
    as old as our mothers and fathers . . .
  steel and smoke,
  technology and arrogance,
  hate birthed of oppression,
  violence all around,
  violence all around . . . and flesh . . . torn flesh,
                       burned flesh,
                       crushed flesh,
                       lost flesh,
  steel against flesh, fire searing skin,
  disorder, chaos, confusion, rage, bottomless anxiety.
And we come equipped by our fathers and mothers . . .
  with poetry: surging images,
           two lines of candor,
           openings and closings of praise,
           truth-telling imperatives spoken
              toward you,
           imagination all voiced to you,
  poetry held deep midst violence,
  poetry of praise midst rage,
  poetry of lament midst loss,
  poetry as wager against hate.
So we pray as we launch into this poetry,
  soak our lives in it,
  overwhelm us by its old cadences,

speak this poetry on our lips
    that we may echo and shadow and trust many
        mothers and fathers
    for whom this poetry contained the violence.
Utter us through fathers and mothers
    close to You in awe,
    You, the true subject of all our poetry. Amen.

    —September 12, 2001, Columbia Theological Seminary

(One Week after the
World Trade Center Bombing)

When the world spins crazy,
              spins wild and out of control,
              spins toward rage and hate
                and violence,
              spins beyond our wisdom and nearly
                beyond our faith,
When the world spins to chaos as it does now
      among us . . .
We are glad for sobering roots that provide ballast
      in the storm.
So we thank you for our rootage in communities
      of faith,
              for many fathers and mothers
                who have believed and trusted
                as firm witnesses to us,
              for their many stories of wonder,
                awe, and healing.
We are glad this night in this company
              for the rootage of the text
              for its daring testimony,
              for its deep commands,
              for its exuberant tales.

Because we know that as we probe deep into this
text . . . clear to its bottom,
>> we will find you hiding there,
>> we will find you showing yourself there,
>>> speaking as you do,
>>> governing,
>>> healing,
>>> judging.
And when we meet you hiddenly,
> we find the spin not so unnerving,
> because from you the world again has a chance
> for life and sense and wholeness.
We pray midst the spinning, not yet unnerved,
>> but waiting and watching and listening,
>> for you are the truth that contains all our spin.
>> Amen.

— September 17, 2001, Columbia Theological Seminary

(With the World Trade Center in the Background)

The intrusion of pain,
the eruption of anger,
the embrace of rage,
and then bewilderment and wonderment and awe.
Our lives in faith are situated among the poets:
The poet talks about
    swords to plowshears,
    spears to pruning hooks,
    and unlearning war.
But answered by a shadow poet who bids us,
    plowshears to swords,
    pruning hooks to spears,
    be not a weakling! (Joel 3:10)
The poems conflict us, as we are conflicted,
  sensing and knowing better,
  knowing better but yielding.
Do not deliver us from the clashing poems
  that are your word to us.
But give us courage and freedom and faith . . .
    O Prince of Peace. Amen.

—September 18, 2001, Columbia Theological Seminary

(Days after the World Trade Center)

We do not really know about running and hiding.
We do not have any real sense, ourselves,
  of being under assault,
 for we live privileged, safe lives,
 learning in a garden near paradise.
Nonetheless the fear and the prayer
 live close beneath the surface . . .
  enemies we cannot see,
  old threats lingering unresolved from childhood,
  wild stirrings in the night that we cannot control.
And then we line out our imperative petitions,
 frantic . . . at least anxious;
 fearful . . . at least bewildered;
Turning to you, only you, you . . . nowhere else.
In the midst of our anxiety, confidence wells up,
in our present stress, old well-being echoes.

We speak and the world turns confident and grateful,
   not because we believe our own words,
   but because of your presence,
        your powerful, bold, reliable presence
            looms large,
            larger than fear,
            larger than anxiety,
            large enough . . .
            and in our small vulnerability,
                we give thanks.
                        Amen.

   — *September 26, 2001, Columbia Theological Seminary*

(DMin Day 4)

Creator God, we celebrate you:
  You make springs gush forth in the valleys;
  They flow between the hills,
  giving drink to every wild animal,
  the wild asses quench their thirst (Ps. 104:10–11).
You send rain and water the earth,
  it springs to growth,
  we eat and are satisfied,
  we thank you and easily push back from the table.
In our comfortable plenty,
  we notice drought here
    and famine there, the work of human hands.
  The looks seem remote from us,
  but in solidarity we register the loss,
                    and the fear,
                    and the death.
We count on water and rain and growth and bread.
We count on your regularities,
  but then . . . we look for peace, but find no good,
                    for a time of healing,
            but there is terror instead (Jer. 14:19).
We do not expect failed rain,
                or failed bread,
                or failed peace,
                or failed healing.

The failure lies deep in the fabric of our common life.
We turn away from that self-destructiveness . . .
back to you,
>   You . . . creator, beginning and end,
>   first and last,
>   You . . . seedtime and harvest,
>   cold and heat,
>   summer and winter,
>   You . . . whose patience we try.
>   You . . . whose sovereign will for good,
>   overrides our capacity
>   for self-destruction.

Look to this world of need: restore,
>   re-create,
>   enliven,
>   give rain,
>   give food,
>   give peace.

For there is no other source . . .
None except you in your sovereign reliability. Amen.

— *October 25, 2001, Columbia Theological Seminary*

———— ∽∾ ————

Kurt died and was sure he would not go to heaven,
    sure there is no heaven,
     sure there is not a God who might
    govern heaven.

At his death, we dare to enter your presence
  through the prism of his words and his courage.

We recall his tease,
  that prevents us from being too
   serious about ourselves;
We recall his indignation,
  at the way we have made a mockery
     of human dignity;
We recall his irreverence
  as he refused to honor our pieties.

But most of all . . . in your presence . . .
  we recall Dresden and
     Coventry, and
     Auschwitz, and
     Hiroshima, and
     Chernobyl, and
     My Lai (Vietnam), and
     Abu Ghraib.

His Dresden was filled with
  bombs dropped indiscriminately,
  and civilians burned savagely,

and crackling flames and
falling buildings,
and violated culture,
and acres and acres of inhumanity.

His Dresden is so particular . . . as he bore his witness.
But his Dresden is everywhere and continuing,
    in our barbarism as state policy,
    in our eagerness to practice violence
    in the pursuit of control.

He died with the refrain, "So it goes":
    So it goes in Dresden
        and countless other places;
    so it goes with technology linked to ideology;
    so it goes with patriotism linked to oil;
    so it goes with shamelessness
                    redefined as a principle;
    so it goes in life and in death;
    so it goes . . . except that we, unlike Kurt, do not
                    stop with his cynicism.

We dare to veto his randomness
    with "Your kingdom, Your power, and Your glory."
Except, like him, we see few signs of your rule.
We give you thanks for his life and for his testimony,
    and we pray that by your sturdy rule and
        by our deep repentance
        it may yet "go" differently. Amen.
                                    —*April 15, 2007*

We pause at our beginning
    to remember Martin!
  We remember Martin in gratitude
    for his daring speech,
    for his bold dreaming,
    for his bodily courage,
    for his unwavering faith,
    for his savage ending,
    for his irrevocable legacy
        of justice.

We are able to recall through him and with him
  the long-term brutality
        of "the American dilemma,"
        of race and
        of hate and
        of violence,
  and of his hard-fought gains for human rights.

We remember with him
- the brave men and women
  who walked and sang and danced our freedom;
- the parade of victims of racism and injustice;
- the countless ones damaged
  in our deep-rooted violence;
- the frightened, distorted perpetrators
  of violence against human flesh;
- the bold jurists and agents of the law
  who have believed and practiced better.

We remember his role as a drum major,
     and the beat of freedom,
     and the cadence of justice,
     and the tempo of courage.

In our gratitude this night,
   we pray for courage,
     the courage of our baptism,
     sealed as we are as your own,
   to break our cowardly collusions
   that we may, in his wake,
     pray and speak and say and act
       your nonnegotiable newness
     dreamed by you and by him and then by us.
   You beautiful dreamer! Amen.

> *—January 21, 2008, Martin Luther King Jr. Day,*
> *January Adventure, St. Simons Island*

It is not difficult to pray in Atlanta these days,
  especially if one is white and educated and working.
There is so much to appreciate in the city,
      money to be made,
      art to enjoy,
      teams to cheer,
      music to hear,
      jobs of many kinds . . . well-paying.

But this city too busy to hate
  has become, alas, a city too busy to remember.

We take our task of faith this day in this city of amnesia
  to remember . . .
  to remember the hurtful days of riot
          a century ago,
  to remember the fear and the hate
    and the violence and the shame.

In all this, Atlanta is not much better or much worse
  than a hundred other cities of fear and hate.
But it is our city.
  And in our city there are still residues of
    the old stuff we dare not forget,
    the old stuff of ill-distributed wealth,
      and unequal health care,
      and privileged schools amid mediocre ones,
      and project housing that still separates
        rich and poor,
        partly by color, and partly by ethnicity.

We remember without glossing over,
    and imagine frightened children,
    and burning streets,
    and inflammatory newspapers,
    and lack of courageous vision.

We remember and we hope . . .
    We hope to have learned,
            and to have forgiven,
            and to have resolved "never again."

Finally we pray your blessing on this city,
    that we might be forgiven,
    that we might remember,
    that we might commit afresh
        to the common good,
        to the sharing of resources,
        to the enhancement of neighbor,
        to the welcoming of the other,
    that our city, here and now, might be a
        visible venue for your way in the world.

We pray in the name of Jesus who wept over his
own city. Amen.

—September 22, 2006

God as mother, God as father to us,
   We are glad to be "at home" with you;
   We are glad to be with sisters and brothers,
      here and everywhere;
   We are glad for the promise you make to us for an
      alternative life in the world;
   We are glad for the expectation you have of us,
      that calls us beyond ourselves to
      your large purposes for the world.
We come to thank you for the goodness
      of our lives in your presence,
   For the daily gifts of food and clothing and
      shelter that we so take for granted,
   For the presence of good, caring neighbors
      who call us by name;
   For the deep assurances of belonging
      that let us be at ease in your presence.
We come to you pledged in loyalty,
   That we take your purposes as our purposes,
   We thank you for your will for peace,
      and we pledge to be peacemakers;
   We thank you for our dreams of justice,
      and we pledge to be at work for justice
      in the world;
   We thank you for your endless gifts
      of mercy, compassion, and gentleness,
      and we promise to be practitioners
        of your generous arts.

We do not come before you alone;
    We come with all sorts and conditions of humankind
        who are our neighbors.
    So we pray your mercy with the sick
        and the dying;
    We seek your attentiveness to the poor
        and the needy;
    We hold up for you the anxious and the fearful,
        the brutalized and those who brutalize.
We do not always sense your attentiveness
        to the needs around us;
    So we address you firmly,
        and expect you to be at work
            toward your kingdom
            before our very eyes.
We dare to pray these things
        because we are followers of Jesus.
    And now we echo his best prayer toward you:
Our Father . . .

*—June 7, 2009, First Congregational United Church of
Christ, Hendersonville, North Carolina*

We pray with, and
      for, and
      on behalf of, and
      alongside
         the white comers who have occupied
         the entire land.
We remember the mixed motivations
with which we came to the new land;
  we came for economic opportunity,
    after the exhausted work of our ancient lands;
  we came for religious freedom,
    and promptly imposed our religion on others;
  we came with religious zeal,
    believing we were as commissioned
      as was Joshua before us
        to seize "the empty land."
We remember that with a mix of pride for our success,
    and with shame for our habit of brutality.
When we arrived, we were surprised to find them here
    long ahead of us.
  We traded with our new friends and were honest;
  we bargained with our new competitors and
    conned them when we could;
  we assaulted our new enemies who resisted us,
    and used whatever force was necessary
      until we displaced them,
      until we occupied their hunting spaces,
      and confined them like prisoners in places
      of hopelessness.

And now with great measures of honesty,
    and with deep waves of chagrin,
    we find that we cannot undo our earlier violence,
    nor do we want to lose what we have come to
        possess.
So we pray for a strong gift of grace,
    to break the vicious cycles of violence, abuse,
        and exploitation:
    give us enough compassion to value traditions
        other than our own;
    give us enough mercy to entertain and engage
        with cultures other than our own;
    give us enough generosity that we ask
        forgiveness for old sins of confiscation.
Turn, we pray, our legal properties
            into shared inheritance,
    that we may yet become a genuine neighborhood
        of sisters and brothers.
We pray in the name of Jesus to
            forgive our haughty self-regard;
            forgive us in our moment of honesty.
    You are the one who makes new,
    evoking possibilities even among us
        in our exhausted self-sufficiency. Amen.

    — *June 26, 2012, Columbia Theological Seminary*

(On Reading Philippians 2:1–11)

One: We are stunned, holy God, by the courageous obedience of Jesus that contradicted
the rulers of this age and brought him to his
death. By his courageous obedience

All: We are stunned.

One: We are shocked, holy God, that in his hum-
bling emptiness he had power to feed in
abundance, to heal in generosity, and to forgive in compassion. By his emptied power to
feed, heal, and forgive

All: We are shocked.

One: We are amazed, holy God, that you have
given him Easter honor that makes him Lord
of lords, displacing all other lords and kings.
By his Easter fullness

All: We are amazed.

One: We are awed, holy God, that the name of
Jesus evokes honor and glory, dominion and
authority. We are awed.

**All: We are awed with bent knees and doxological
tongues.**

One: We are mindful, holy God, of all the emptiness of those who lack what is needed for a whole life . . . adequate schools, jobs, health care. We see that emptiness all around.

All: **We are mindful of that need and take it as a concern of our lives as we ponder how to care.**

One: We are mindful, holy God, of the flood of Easter fullness that comes to those with courage and energy for obedience. We are aware of many saints among us who live with such Easter fullness.

All: **We give thanks for them as we ourselves ponder joining that wondrous company.**

One: We are mindful, holy God, of those in special need who await your healing, transformative touch and we name them. . . . We name them in confident petition.

All: **We pray for them as we pray for ourselves.**

One: We are thankful, Lord of life, for those who have lived among us and now have died. . . . We name them in gratitude.

All: **We entrust them to your mercy.**

—March 28, 2017, St. Timothy Episcopal Church,
Cincinnati, Ohio

Father of orphans—
  so you are named in the ancient text (Ps. 68:5)—
    You who notices when no one else notices;
    You who treasures when no one else treasures;
    You who guards and protects when no one else
      is vigilant . . .
Mother who never forgets—
  so you are named in the ancient text (Isa. 49:15)—
    You who remembers tots birthed and lost,
    You who aches to nurse and give comfort,
    You who writes down their names indelibly,
    You who never forgets,
    You who champions forgotten children . . .

And we—are so unlike you:
    We are prone to violence in a culture of violence,
      ready for torture and sex crimes
        and abuse of the poor,
    We who have our orgies of hate,
    We who have our sprees of anger,
    We who have our seasons of greed and anxiety,
    All of which leads to our recurring
        carnival of violence.
We are unlike you . . . the father who protects
                        in a culture of violence,
                . . . the mother who remembers
                        in a culture that discards and
                        deletes,
    You in your fidelity and staying power,
    We in our flimsy disregard and indifference.

Before you now we dare three petitions:
- That you be near to those children lost to us,
  To hold them and their families
  in your abiding care,
  That you be near to children at risk,
  to enfold them in safety;
- That you should forgive the perpetrators who
  In a frenzy of rage know not what they do;
  Forgive them even in this culture of revenge
  and retaliation;
- That you should transform us and our culture,
  That we may be a culture of protection
  that pays attention,
  That our thirst for hurt may be curbed
  by a system of laws,
  That mindless violence may be contained
  by a vision of justice
  that attends to the vulnerable,
  That we may become a neighborhood of
  charity and restoration,
  That we reconcile without revenge
  our neighbors and our enemies.

It boggles our minds that we might govern
  as you govern;
  That we might forgive as you forgive;
  That we might notice as you notice;
  That we might hope in you amid our hopelessness;
  That we who are so unlike you
  May become like you in mercy that heals
  and in justice that transforms.

We pray in the vulnerable name of Jesus
   Who invests in your fatherliness,
   Who remembers and cherishes
      like the mother you are,
   Who invites the children to him
      and welcomes them.
We pray in the awareness of his suffering love
   and in the power of his Easter life. Amen.

— Good Friday 2013, Columbia Theological Seminary

We give you thanks for the babe born amid violence.
We give you thanks for the miracle of Bethlehem,
    born in the midst of Jerusalem aggression.

We do not understand why the innocents
        must be slaughtered;
we know that your kingdom comes
        amid violence and travail.
    Our time would be a good time
        for your kingdom to come,
        because we have had enough
            of violence and travail.

We wait with eager longing,
but also with enormous fear,
        because your promises do not coincide
            with our favorite injustices.

We pray for the coming of your kingdom on earth
    even as it is around your heavenly throne,
        with singing, joy, and astonishment.

We are people grown weary of waiting.
We dwell in the midst of cynical people,
    and we have settled for what we can control.

We do know that you hold initiative for our lives,
    that your love planned our salvation
        before we saw the light of day.

We wait for your coming, in your vulnerable baby
through whom all things are made new.

Amen.

—December 6, 1976

Another brutality,
another school killing,
another grief beyond telling . . .
   and loss . . .
        in Colorado,
        in Wisconsin,
        among the Amish.

We are reduced to weeping silence,
   even as we breed a violent culture,
   even as we kill the sons and daughters of
        our "enemies,"
   even as we fail to live and cherish and respect
        the forgotten of our common life.

There is no joy among us as we empty our schoolhouses;
there is no health among us as we move in fear and
        bottomless anxiety;
there is little hope among us as we fall helpless before
   the gunshot and the shriek and the blood
        and the panic;
we pray to you only because we do not know
        what else to do.

So we pray, move powerfully in our body politic,
        move us toward peaceableness
           that does not want to hurt or to kill,
        move us toward justice
           that the troubled and the forgotten
             may know mercy,
        move us toward forgiveness
           that we may escape the trap of
           revenge.

Empower us to turn our weapons to acts of mercy,
        to turn our missiles to gestures of
           friendship,
        to turn our bombs to policies of
           reconciliation;

and while we are turning,
   hear our sadness,
       our loss,
       our bitterness.

We dare to pray our needfulness to you
   because you have been there on that
       gray Friday,
       and watched your own Son be murdered
          for "reasons of state."

Good God . . . do Easter!
  Here and among these families,
  here and in Iraq,
  here and in all our places of brutality.

Move our Easter grief now . . .
  without too much innocence . . .
  to your Sunday joy.
We pray in the one crucified and risen
    who is our Lord and Savior. Amen.

—October 4, 2006

We enjoyed the fleshpots,
    The amber waves of grain,
        All the well-being
            wealth and smarts could produce.
And then, in rage, bewilderment, violence,
    We lost it all,
    We lost our place and our power,
    We settled into fear and displacement,
    We were hammered until we lost everything.
We fled and were hemmed in . . .

                until we lost everything.
We sat by the waters and wept,
            by the River Potomac;
            by the River Delaware;
            by the River Hudson;
            by the River Ohio;
            by the River Mississippi.
        We wept our losses:
            In our sadness, we said to the empire
                that passed us by:
    Is it nothing to you, all you who pass by?
    Look and see
        if there is any sorrow like my sorrow,
            which was brought upon me.
And we grieve yet.
But we grieve as those who hope:
    We hope for the recovery of the well-being
        we have lost.
    We do not hope for recovery of our land.

But we do hope . . . and pray,
  for recovery of our social status,
  for new just treatment of us as first-class citizens;
  for economic viability;
  for respect for our tribal traditions as serious as
    European rootage,
  for the grace to forgive and be reconciled.
We pray with treasured memories;
We pray with unabated grief.
We pray with deep and steady hope.
  We pray, come, Spirit, and make new . . .
    In the name of Jesus who gives life. Amen.

                —*June 26, 2012, Columbia Theological Seminary*

(On Reading Amos 8:4–8)

We have been summoned forever to "listen"
    since the first *Shema'* of Moses (Deut. 6:4).
We were not sure whom the poet addressed;
    But then he specified:
        you who trample,
        you who ruin the poor,
        you who eagerly rush to exploitative business
            or exploitative sports,
        you who rig the scales,
            and cheat the poor with weights,
            and leverage interest rates,
            and manipulate tax laws,
            and do wage theft when you can.
We did not think it pertained to us, we good people,
    because we did not notice, we did not look carefully,
    we did not recognize our own participation,
    we do not think systemically about how
        our benefit is enmeshed in such subtle violence.
But the poet knows:
    the poet saw that the poor are had cheap;
    the poet laid out how we treat the poor in cheap ways,
        how we push chaff as grain,
        how we cut corners with the vulnerable,
            creating food deserts
            and failed schools,
            and flawed services all around.

The poet did not quibble;
he saw and spoke the raw hard truth.
He saw that we wanted no sabbath from profit,
                    no rest from exploitation,
                    no break from self-fulfillment
                        at the expense of others,
                    no slack in shopping
                        or entertainment
                        or indulgence.
He saw that our self-celebration vetoed
the old command of sabbath, because
    we could not wait,
    we could not pause,
    we could not put off success and growth and
        wealth and domination.
In response,
    the poet offers us words from God
        who is not mocked,
    from the holy One who sees through
        our fake piety.
What words they are!!!
    The creator of heaven and earth notices
        our wee self-serving maneuvers;
    The Lord of history takes note and will not forget
        as the evidence piles up.
And the outcome of our unacknowledged
shenanigans returned to us by the holy God??

The news is not good,
even if given in terrifying poetic imagery:
> The land trembles in destabilization; who knew?
> A big sadness comes among us; who anticipated?
> A force of chaos like a rising tide; who was ready?
> Floodwaters of disorder;
>> who could tread that much water?

We could call it an act of God,
> or an environmental crisis,
> or a loss of safety:
>> A world order under threat?
>> A violent society?
>> A failed economy?
>> A lethal ecology?

All because we have rushed through sabbath;
we could not wait.
> We could not take time to be holy,
>> because holiness, amid the rough-and-tumble
>>> of the real world,
>>>> will not get us a cup of coffee. Amen.

We are in free fall:
    We are bewildered about our economy,
            losing houses and jobs;
    We are anxious about our moral infrastructure
        and losing our neighborliness;
    We are appalled at the violence
        and losing our sense of safety;
    We are adrift about the future of the church
        and the loss of our sense of the normal.

We are in free fall:
    Tonight we will watch and listen
        for scenarios of our future;
    We will hear about government
        as a reliable safety net;
    We will learn about the market
        as our last best hope;
    We will hear truth and slogans;
    We will watch images and constructed reality;
    We will invest our best provisional hope
        according to our vested interests.
But when we are done and turn off the set,
    the ghosts of disorientation will still be strong
        in the land.

From the free fall not yet to its bottom,
we reach toward you
    and address you.
  You are our safety net;
  You are our comfort in this age
    and in the age to come;
  You are our summons to deep newness.
Our life is about you,
  and then about our neighbor,
    and finally about ourselves.
Hear us amid the free fall:
  Bottom us out in new possibility
  according to your faithful mercy. Amen.

—October 3, 2012, St. Timothy Episcopal Church,
Cincinnati, Ohio

Living Word, we walk up to these holy words in eagerness, hoping for a message of love. We walk up to these holy words in trepidation, aware that your truth might be offered among us. We walk up to these holy words along with many Jewish, Christian, and Muslim sisters and brothers who also come in eagerness and trepidation. We pray for ears beyond our comfort zone, that we might hear what your Spirit is saying to the church. Amen.

—August 27, 2017, St. Timothy Episcopal Church, Cincinnati, Ohio

(Deuteronomy)

We know the list well . . .
   Widow, orphan, immigrant, poor!

We know the list in many configurations:
   orphan, poor, widow, immigrant;
   immigrant, widow, poor, orphan;
   poor, orphan, immigrant, widow.

They loom large among us . . .
     we are surrounded by them!

We know, as well, that they loom large for you . . .
   You are attentive to them.
   We pray to you, being surrounded as we are,
   Draw us away from our privilege,
          from our entitlements,
          from our advantage.
   By this hard scroll,
     Disrupt our advantage.

You redirect our energies,
   You refocus our futures,
   You bind us to your well-beloved neighbors.

And we hear cadences,
   concerning
      the "least" to be fed
                  and visited
                  and cared for,
   even while we prattle on about
                  pensions, and
                  income, and
                  interest, and
                  investment.
You summon us through this scroll,
   And change our agenda.
Give us this day,
   the grace to be changed by the scroll,
   that we may notice, remember, and acknowledge,
   perhaps to move into vulnerability,
   toward your new rule. Amen.

   —*October 30, 2008, Columbia Theological Seminary,*
                              DMin Day 9

Holy God:
> There is no good fit between your promises
>> and our need.
> There is no neat matchup between your graciousness
>> and the injustice
>> that stalks our world.

We are on both sides of injustice:
> we suffer from it, and we victimize others.
>> We know the groans of oppression, and
>> we know the hard-heartedness
>>> of being oppressors.

We cannot on our own break the cycles
in our lives or in our city.
So we pray, as our mothers and fathers
have always prayed,
> that you would come mightily, and
> that you would make all things new.

We are aware of the deaths that are being died
in our culture, and
> of the cries of distress that must be cried.

We also know your promises of joy;
We know in Jesus of Nazareth that engagement
with injustice is transformative.
> May it be so among us.

Come among us, according to your good purposes.
Amen.

—October 22, 1976

We pray for the energy of Jesus to be
    at work in our community.
The cry of his homelessness summons us to be
    aware of the homeless-making of our society.
We are undone by where we find ourselves
and yet it is a gift to come down where we ought to be.

We pray for more wisdom and more courage
    than we have,
in order to face our common calling
    and to be free enough
to live toward your promises of justice and peace for all
our brothers and sisters.

We pray in the joy, the buoyancy, and the anguish of
Jesus of Nazareth.

Amen.

—November 12, 1976

(On Reading Exodus 20:17)

Our master rabbi told a tale of building bigger barns, to store more grain to have more stuff, because the man did not have enough yet. Before he told the tale, he said simply, "Be on guard against all covetousness" (Luke 12:15). Or we translate "greed":

"Be on your guard against all kinds of greed,
for one's life does not consist
in the abundance of possessions."

When Jesus said that, he appealed back to Moses at Sinai. Via Moses at Sinai, we received ten lordly words. The first word was about the worship of things: "No graven images" (Exod. 20:4–6).
The tenth is: Do not covet;

Do not be greedy;

Do not be acquisitive;

Do not accumulate;

Do not hunger and thirst for more.

The Lord of Sinai has set limits:

Do not covet your neighbor's house;

Do not covet your neighbor's wife;

Do not covet what belongs
to your neighbor.

Do not covet . . . and then three times,
neighbor,
neighbor,
neighbor.

We live, each of us and all of us,
    in an economy of coveting:
        The tax and mortgage laws are designed
            to let the powerful accumulate more;
        The ads are designed to make us desire
            what we do not need;
        The out-of-control military is designed to protect
            unsustainable advantage of things in the world;
        The ecological threat is the result of cravings
            that violate the limit of sustainable creation.
The tax laws, the TV ads, the strong military,
the ruin of creation,
    all serve to impinge harmfully
        upon the neighborhood.
        The tax and mortgage laws prey
            upon vulnerable neighbors;
        The ads seduce us to value things
            as substitutes for relationships;
        The military ideology turns neighbors
            into enemies;
        The exploitation of the earth refuses to reckon
            with rabbits and radishes
            as neighbors.

But we have known better since Sinai!
We know, when we do sabbath pause,
that we can live well
        without an updated computer or phone;
        without another new car;
        without elective cosmetic surgery;
        without remedial drugs, etc., etc., etc.

We cannot and have no deep desire
to live without neighbors.
We confess our anxiety about scarcity,
    about not yet having enough and being left behind.
We confess, when we do sabbath pause,
    that we do not treasure neighbor enough,
        the one close at hand;
        the one far away;
        the one who shows mercy;
        the one who needs mercy.
We pledge in your presence,
greater resolve for sabbath,
    that we may submit our restless anxiety
        to your alternative future,
    that we may refocus our lives in your gracious will,
    that we may trade coveted things
        for treasured neighbors,
    that we may come to our true selves,
        liberated from the tyranny for more.
At sundown on sabbath,
we will gladly and loudly declare,
"Free at last!" Amen.

Holy God, since you first spoke to your people,
you have spoken promises of freedom
and dreams of justice.
Those promises have scarcely come to reality.

We confess you to be at work in our world and
we give you thanks for every crack where freedom
breaks through.
We praise your name for every coming of justice
in small ways among us.

We do, indeed, work both sides of the street. We are
people who are oppressed—and it makes us angry. We
are people who oppress—and it makes us tired.

We thank you for brave men and women who will not
leave the world organized against you.

We thank you for suffering and for painful ways in
which your healing comes among us.

We hold in your presence this day all those who
believe your promises and dream your dreams.

We wait with eager and sure longing for the kingdom
that you have promised.

Amen.

—November 19, 1976

You, good creator, are the *alpha point* of all
of our life and our faith.

And now we ponder that you are not only author
and pioneer, but you also are the completer
and finisher, our *omega point*.
In this day of an ending, we ponder
how to pray and how to end.

We might pray amid exiled
powers that dream of restoration.

We might pray amid exiles
who know themselves to be
the wave of your future.

We might pray in hope while we
watch empires
tread water and sink into oblivion.

We might pray with the scroll
in our hand, at the
ready for testimony.

We are given to many modes of prayer,
each of which suits our season of hope.

All our prayers are that our endings
    should be, as was our beginning,
    according to your purpose.

We submit our work and our living as
    sacrifice to you. We end our time in
    thanksgiving,
            grateful for our common vocation;
            glad for each other;
            thankful for new learnings and
                    fresh work to do.

Travel us safely home, and bless the church
    where we will go again, that in our
    local place you may receive our
    fresh thanks and our glad obedience. Amen.

(On Reading Psalm 73)

We have signed on with you . . .
    As we say, "Sealed as Christ's own forever."
We are glad for it.
We understand . . . we have signed on
        For neighbor love;
        For forgiveness of our enemies;
        For hospitality even when we are afraid;
        For generosity even when we run short;
        For guidance by your Spirit even when we
            know better.

We have signed on, but with a short attention span;
    We notice other ways to live,
        And we tilt toward them:
    Instead of neighbor love, love of self
        and of our kind is preferable;
    Instead of forgiveness of enemies, we prefer
        staying wounded and holding grudges;
    Instead of hospitality, we lock down everything;
    Instead of generosity, we look to
        our own interest;
    Instead of guidance, we hold to
        our own assured way.
We are left double-minded
        About your welcome of us
        And our preference of otherwise.

And then, beyond ourselves,
    We are wooed back to you, or
    We are summoned back to you, or
    We are jerked back to you.
And we are glad, because
    Being your own forever
        Is the truth of our life
            And our deepest joy.
Back with you is our best way in the world. Amen.

—October 22, 2014, St. Timothy Episcopal Church,
Cincinnati, Ohio

Every week in your kingdom is brotherhood week.
Every day in your rule is sisterhood day.
    We live by and for our brothers.
    We live from and toward our sisters.
And we thank you for the good company of kinfolk
    to whom you have bound us.

But alas!
    Our good connections are so much
        disrupted and disordered,
        By nightmares of scarcity and
        hopes for more land and more oil
        and more beer and more sex;

        By dreams of getting ahead and
            controlling and dominating;

        By gestures that rob brother or sister
           of time or space,
           or energy or goods . . .
           for the sake of our betterment.

We are fractured folk in the family,
    and we posture too much,
        bowing down or
        being bowed down to.

So we pray, amid our study,
   refurbish the human fabric,
   rehabilitate the great family of man,
   and the great retinue of women,
that we may gather in wonder, love, and praise,
      in your self-giving presence,
      unafraid,
      neither hurt nor hurting. Amen.

—March 6, 2008, Columbia Theological Seminary
Exegesis Class

One: In your presence we do not doubt that the
truth will make us free.
Here we are, Lord of heaven, good people
enmeshed in systems of oppression that
we did not design,
where too many are excluded by class,
race, or gender,
where too many children lack food,
where too many are left behind in
hopeless poverty,
even amid our wealth.
Be the God of truth among us,

All: that we may be freed.

One: Here we are, Lord of earth, good people,
benefiting from a system of exploitation,
sustained by cheap labor on our behalf,
engaged in advantages that are lawful
but unjust,
enjoying benefits given us, but unseen
and unacknowledged.
Be the God of truth among us,

All: that we may be freed.

One: Here we are, Lord of our political economy,
      good people
          colluding in systems of injustice,
              not noticing the ways in which top-down
                  decisions yield unbearable
                      outcomes below,
              not seeing how the dots of power
                  are connected,
              and mostly not wanting to see
                  those connections.
      Be the God of truth among us,
All: that we may be freed.

One: Here we are, Lord Jesus, your faithful
          followers,
          baptized into your movement,
          signed on as disciples,
          but with little discipline,
          responsive to your summons.
      Be the God of truth among us,
All: that we may be freed.

One: Here we are, Lord Jesus, sheep of your flock,
          ready to be led anew,
          prepared to act out our baptism,
          glad for your calling to us.
      Be the God of truth among us,
All: that we may be freed.

One: Here we are, healing Spirit of God,
　　　bringing before you those near and dear to us
　　　who face toil and tribulation,
　　　wound and loss . . .
　　Be the God of healing truth among us,

All: that we may be whole.

One: Here we are, Spirit of life who has defeated
　　　the power of death,
　　　naming our dear dead before you . . .
　　Be the God of new life among us,

All: that we may be comforted . . .

*—August 20, 2017, St. Timothy Episcopal Church,
Cincinnati, Ohio*

We are covenant makers:
>We make all kinds of vows, oaths, and promises,
>We commit ourselves and practice fidelity,
>We sign on for obedience.

We sign on seriously, but also casually and too easily.
We find ourselves, too soon and too often,
>allied with earthliness: We pant after commodities,
>>We look for quick fixes.
>>We lust after pure
>>well-being.

We look our partners in the face,
>staring at us too often is death, as partner,
>our partner too often too dread-filled to bear.

And then you come, our true and only partner,
>You snatch us from deathliness,
>you nullify our phony covenants,
>and invite us to our proper fidelity.

We look back in wonderment to deathly partners
overcome by you.
We look forward in joy to life with you.
We are betwixt and between what was in earthliness
and what will be in new life;
In that moment of turn,
>we glimpse life with you,
>>life simple, joyous, obedient,
>>demanding all, not too much,
>>but all. Amen.

— *October 30, 2001, Columbia Theological Seminary*

(On Reading Acts 3:1–16)

You God who raises the dead;
You God who gives life;
You God who heals;
Dear Sir:
Here we are in the waiting room of your presence,
hoping for an appointment. We come with our sev-
eral diseases and disabilities,

    diseases of feet and arms and legs and digestive tracts,
    disabilities of body and of spirit,

      lame in a thousand ways.

Here we sit and wait, with great expectation.
    We expect and hope for healing from you,

               for transformation,

               for forgiveness,

               for emancipation.

    We expect . . . because we have heard tales
    of your healing capacity,

      old stories of lepers healed and women
        with bad backs,

      new reports of beggars who ask for alms
        and receive healing.

Here we are, waiting for you,
But we do not wait alone:

    We bring as our companions in suffering
      the folk in this congregation who wait
        in need and in hope.

    We bring as our companions the wretched who wait,
      diseased by economic disadvantage,

disabled by political exclusionary power,
immobilized by a thousand slaveries
and a dozen anxieties,
alienated by failures and other open sores.
We bring as our companions the complacent
who discover too late that they have grown
numb in indifference,
and cannot move their hands to help,
or their hearts to connect.
We bring as our companions
the nations of the world that are not healed,
the frightened nations armed to their teeth,
the old colonial powers that still want
to control oil and markets,
the erstwhile colonies that still lack viability,
and our own nation-state with its pathologies
of greed and hate and violence.
We are all here before you,
not doubting your capacity,
waiting for your readiness,
open to your prescriptions,
ready immediately to leap and run in health,
to dance and sing
in restoration,
to praise you in our newness.
Dear Doctor: deal with us soon,
bring your best arts of newness,
and make all things new,
even here,
even now,
even for us. Amen.

—April 23, 2012

We are fully settled as Easter people.
　　We confess: Christ has died,
　　　　　　　　　Christ has risen.
　　We wait for the resurrection of the body
　　　　　　　　　and the life everlasting.
All this from you, God of life.

But in the stillness between our creedal syllables,
　　we hear weeping children,
　　　　standing by burned homes and dead parents;
　　we hear weeping mothers,
　　　　at loss with their dead soldier sons;
　　we hear the stillness of death
　　　　in our environment where not even micely
　　　　　　creatures stir.

We are witnesses to death . . .
　　More than that, we crave death:
　　　　death to our enemies,
　　　　death to the poor who lack coverage,
　　　　death to the criminals who exasperate us,
　　　　death to our rain forests and oceans,
　　　　all on the assumption that such deaths
　　　　　　make us safer.

We know better but fall for it anyway.
　We wish for better eyes to weep, and
　　better tears to shed, and
　　better grief to moan,
　to be honest about the dying and the killing
　　and the loss.

But then, caught short by your Easter power,
　　give us courage to choose life,
　　give us freedom to face down death,
　　give us energy to dance and laugh Easter,
　for we do say with a full heart . . .
　　　Christ is risen,
　　　He is risen indeed. Amen.

　　　— January 9, 2008, Columbia Theological Seminary
　　　　　　　　　　　　　　　　　　　DMin Class

We are a near-violent company,
　　and we dwell in the midst of a violent people.
For this day, given us and our people,
　　we have drawn close to you.
We have pondered your will for justice,
　　　　　　　　　your purpose of well-being,
　　　　　　　　　your impulse toward safety,
　　　　　　　　　your habit of mercy and
　　　　　　　　　　compassion,
　　　　　　　　　your readiness for faithfulness.
We draw close to your resolve,
　　but we ground our lives in your actions.
　　You are the one who rescues and delivers,
　　　　　　　　　who saves and heals,
　　　　　　　　　who reconciles and makes new,
　　　　　　　　　who builds and plants.
We recite your acts, we glory in them, and
　　we see the outcomes of your transformative work.
　　Your ways of acting are a mystery to us,
　　　　　　but we do not doubt.
And we . . . we are made in your image.
　　We live and move in your wake.
　　and so after you;
　　we practice your habits of justice,
　　　　　　　　　your well-being,
　　　　　　　　　your safety,
　　　　　　　　　your mercy and your compassion,
　　　　　　　　　your faithfulness.

And so, after you, we will act:
   We will act to rescue and deliver the vulnerable.
   We will save and heal the forgotten.
   We will reconcile victims and perpetrators,
      and watch for your newness to emerge.
   We will plant policies of generosity,
      and build institutions of sustenance.
   We will live in the circle of our life that is marked
      by Easter buoyancy.
We will do more than recite:
   We will act,
   and create,
   and make new.
As we do that, we will be in the glad company
of your good Son, Jesus.
   He is the one through whom the blind receive
                                 their sight,
                        the lame walk,
                        the lepers are
                                 cleansed,
                        the deaf hear,
                        the dead are raised,
                        the poor have good
                              news brought
                              to them.
He is the one who has broken the force of violence
   and we need not any longer participate in it.

As we draw close to you, to your will and to your acts,
  We receive your Spirit;
  We are blown beyond ourselves toward newness;
  We are empowered to boldness;
  We are energized to staying power.
And we are grateful!
We are grateful for newness that may come through us,
  but surely from you. Amen.

—March 9, 2013, for National Cathedral

Here we are in Epiphany on the way to Lent;
   here we are in Epiphany —
        with a reach to the Gentiles,
        with a reach beyond ourselves,
        with a reach to those unlike us,
          with your love and justice.

Here we are on the way to Lent;
   the way to the cross of contradiction,
   the way to the trial . . .
        before the priests,
        before the governor,
        before the hard men
   who want to stop the news of newness.

We are children of Epiphany in the reach,
we are children of Lent with its Friday stress.

Here we are, on the way back home,
        back to business as usual,
        back to anxiety and stress and requirement,
        back to our loved ones
          and those not easy to love.

We are on our way
        going just as we came,
        going differently because we have been here,
        we have been with each other,
        we have been before you
          in honesty and in joy.

Hold us in your transformative love;
        hold us in your demanding justice;
        hold us deep in your compassion,
that we may live for the neighborhood in new ways,
bound as we are together in the neighborhood,
        all of us together,
            rich and poor,
            young and old,
            beautiful and bruised,
        all of us . . . before you.

You are creator.
You are savior.
You are hovering spirit.
        We will, we pledge,
            travel in your newness. Amen.

—January 23, 2008, January Adventure, St. Simons
Island

TWO

PRAYERS OF
THOU JUSTICE

You are the God from whom no secret can be hid.

You are the God of truth
   to whom the truth must be told.

And so we bring to you
   the truth of the world:
      the truth of hunger and poverty,
      the truth of need and abandonment and anxiety,
      the truth of hurt and dying,
      the truth of violence and war.

All these truths we submit to your more
   powerful life-giving truth.

So we bid you, truth-doing God,
   veto the hunger and poverty in our world,
   override the need and abandonment and anxiety
      so palpable among us,
   cancel out the hurt and the dying
      so pervasive in our world,
   move peaceably against violence
      and enact your *shalom*
         in the face of our threats of war.

We do not hold back from you
    the truth of our need.

Do not hold back from us
    the gospel truth of your mercy
                      compassion and
                      forgiveness.

Sway us from our deep distortion
    into your deep goodness
    that we and our world may again,
      by your verdict,
      be "very good." Amen.

    —September 19, 2002, Columbia Theological Seminary

We are always "fresh from the word."
   You call the worlds into being.
   You call us into your church.
   You call nations and kingdoms to do your will.
   You call swords to plowshears, and
            spears to pruning hooks.
Your calling word is carried, concretely, bodily,
   by your speakers who dare break the world
     by utterance.
   And so we give you thanks,
     for preachers and poets,
     for prophets and writers and editors,
       voices of truth,
       voices of pain,
       voices of alarm and of comfort . . .
the ones who call the world back
to your truthful presence.
We live in a land of silence, denial, and self-sufficiency
   where the word is scarce, and
     ears are grown thick with protective wax
       and heavy skin.
And then your word!
   uttered to us,
   perhaps eventually uttered by us
     in courage and in candor,
   your word given vulnerable and lean,
   your word embodied in Jesus,
   your word incarnated here and there among us,
     at risk.

And we, in our anxiety
    at best pray for fresh ears to hear,
        for quivering lips to speak as you will us to do.
            Amen.

—*February 21, 2002, Columbia Theological Seminary*

———— ∽∽ ————

You: giver,
     father,
     lord,
     judge,
     watcher.
You . . . and we come to terms with you,
          in praise,
          in obedience,
          in gratitude,
          in love.
You . . . and we come to terms poorly,
even like these ancients:
          in disregard,
          in recalcitrance,
          in autonomy,
          in narcissism,
          in forgetting.
You . . . and we wonder why the earth trembles,
          why the world totters,
          why the nations rage.
You . . . be you today in all your you-ness
   and we sign on, feebly, yet again,
      to be your people. Amen.

—*September 11, 2001, Columbia Theological Seminary*

(On Reading Isaiah 1)

We prattle about your sovereignty . . .
      especially we Calvinists;
  all about all things working together for good,
  all about your watchful care and your severe mercies.
And then we are drawn up short;
  by terror that strikes us, in our privilege, as insane;
  by violence that shatters our illusions of well-being;
  by death that reminds us of our at-risk mortality;
  by smoke and fire that have the recurring smell
    of the ovens.
We are bewildered, undone, frightened,
  and then intrude the cadences of these old poets:
    the cadences of fidelity and righteousness;
    the sounds of justice and judgment;
    the images of Sodom and Gomorrah;
    the imperatives of widows and orphans.
Even on such a day we are not minded to yield
on your sovereignty,
  We are, we confess, sobered, put off, placed in dread,
    that you are lord as well as friend,
    that you are hidden as well as visible,
    that you are silent as well as reassuring.
You are our God. That is enough for us . . . but just
barely. We pray in the name of the wounded flesh of
Jesus. Amen.

—September 11, 2001, Columbia Theological Seminary

"Thine alabaster cities gleam,
undimmed by human tears."
We sing unthinkingly of gleaming, alabaster cities,
   We look up *alabaster*,
    ... "a variety of hard calcite,"
   no help there, and we do not linger,
   but settle for *gleaming*:
      bright, shiny steel,
      lights on twenty-four hours a day,
      swift elevators that whisk to the top,
      business, productivity, success, security,
       power . . .
"Pause" . . . undimmed by human tears . . .
   and now dimmed: dimmed by tears,
              blinded by fears,
              wrenched by hate,
              driven by violence,
                 very little alabaster,
                 even less gleaming,
                 lots of tears that dim,
And smoke,
   ashes,
   bodies,
   stench,
   wreckage,
A strange fate for gleaming alabaster.

The great, good cities reduced,
    penultimately we ponder enemies,
    ultimately we are pushed back
      to you,
        you behind every gleam and every alabaster;
        you behind every ash and every corpse;
        you behind every rage and every tear;
        you finally, keeping watch, hidden;
YOU, never to be confused with
      our gleaming alabaster;
YOU, never reduced to our ash and death;
YOU, living God;
YOU, Easter God;
YOU. Amen.

       —October 10, 2001, Columbia Theological Seminary

Ruler of the nations,
dispatcher of empires,
evoker of war,
Father of the Prince of Peace:
We pray for peace,
   even while we are implicated in the violence,
   even while we respond to terror,
   even while we critique our own policies, and
                 pay our taxes, and
                 blush not at "collateral damage."
We pray for peace.
   We are wont to pray for peace on our terms,
                 without inconvenience,
                 without self-criticism;
   We are wont to pray for peace in our time,
                 so as to be
                 neither anxious
                 nor uncomfortable.
We do not, however, pray for peace on any
of our own terms,
But on your terms, in your time, and in your way.
   Keep your promises,
   hold to your vision,
   bring your newness . . . cross-shaped,
for we trust you and wait for you,
   even while we hope and work against the violence.
Act, Lord of peace;
Act soon among us;
Act yourself, and we will give you thanks. Amen.

—November 8, 2001, Columbia Theological Seminary

You, you alone are our news.
We wait for "good tidings,"
   and your tidings are very good indeed.
Our hearing is less good; we are inundated with
"other news."
   CNN gives us liberal news that is not good.
   FOX gives us conservative news that is not good.
   CNN is twiddle,
   FOX is twaddle,
     and everything stays the same after the news . . .
       dark,
       dreary,
       stale,
       static,
       fatigued,
       at the edge of despair.

So be news to us this day,
   news of sight to the blind,
   news of healing for the lepers,
   news of freedom for prisoners,
   news of life for the dying,
   news of emancipation for the poor.
And for ourselves . . . news of well-being,
                security,
                energy,
                a larger vision,
                a deeper vocation.

You are our news. We will listen past the static all day long. Come, good news, fleshed! Amen.

—November 13, 2001, Columbia Theological Seminary

We pause in your presence, God of peace and justice.
We watch while violence stalks strong,
> stomping down what is human and lovely,
> raping what is flowered and innocent,
> burning what stands too large,
> crushing what is weak and vulnerable.
In our safe place we know only a little of violence,
> read about it,
> meet it seldom.
But you know about violence:
> You are the watcher of nations and notice all;
> You know about swords and spears,
> and bombs and missiles . . .
>> and a void of pruning hooks.
Indeed, you are implicated too much in violence,
> working your own wrath,
> endorsing too much hate with faith too deep.
And then we Friday you, as you have Fridayed Jesus.
And we dare say midst the suffering,
> prince of peace,
> lover of the world,
> maker of heaven and earth . . .
>> Cease the Unmaking all around us,
>> In the Friday name of Jesus. Amen.

—December 3, 2001, Columbia Theological Seminary

Our lives are writ large in the story of our time . . .
- lots of money,
- lots of power,
- a large sense of entitlement and privilege,
      the bombs bursting in air.
And in the midst of that, we set our lives down in this
    odd narrative of this odd Jesus.
We draw very close to that tale today,
    and recognize its familiar cadences:
- a story of arrest and policy brutality,
    and we know about that.
- a tale of betrayal and the breaking of trust,
    and we know about that.
- a narrative of denial and cover-up,
    and we know about that . . .
discovering that the story is all about our lives
as it is about his.
And then . . . before our very eyes . . .
while we watched . . .

    He took bread and blessed and broke and gave;
            it was broken and nourishing.
    He took wine and poured it out;
            it was poured out and quenching.

Our story about money and power and entitlement
and privilege is contradicted
   by this odd Thursday gesture.
   So we pray that by sundown today,
   you will make us sons of this broken bread,
   you will make us daughters of this wine poured out.
Thursday us toward the pain of Friday loss. Amen.

   —*March 28, 2002, Columbia Theological Seminary*

We confess you to be creator of heaven and earth
    and we are *awed* by what we have
    seen of your immense power.

We confess you to be the Savior of Israel
    and we stand *under your commands*
    of justice and righteousness.

We confess you to be the Father
of our Lord Jesus Christ
    and we rely on *your deep mercy*
    toward us all.

Hear us as we confess *our awe* before you:
    for mountains and streams,
    snow and ice and lakes,
    lovely in measure,
    beautiful in your framing.

So awed are we that even our
    privilege and jadedness are broken by
    your splendor.

Hear us as we acknowledge before you our
    resolve *to be obedient to your commands*,
    that we shall grow in generosity and forgiveness,
    that we shall practice your reconciling
        justice in concrete and nameable ways,
    that we shall be your way of compassion
        in the world.

Hear us as we *entrust to your care*
    the deepest places of need in our world:
    we pray for peace and justice —
        you lover of the world —
    we pray for peace even while our nation
        is enmeshed in all of the violence of war,
    for peace in every troubled place.

We pray for the dying,
    even as we most of the time assume our
        own immortality.

We pray for the sick.
We pray for pastors and teachers,
        priests and bishops,
            and all who lead your church.

We pray for our own churches,
    that your word may be uttered and
        fleshed on this holy day.

For ourselves we pray safety and well-being,
    for our families your mercy.
        We are *awed* and *obedient*
        committed to your mercy
            reliant *on your mercy*.
            Come and be merciful among us
                all this day long. Amen.

                                    —July 28, 2002, Banff

You addressed our ancient ones, "You and your king…"
You addressed them critically,
             dismissively,
             contemptuously,
And they continued to value what you dismissed.
And now we imagine your same utterance toward us,
             critically,
             dismissively,
             contemptuously:
             You and your king,
             You and your system,
             You and your unrivaled power,
             You and your violence,
             You and your devouring market,
             You and your treasured
                 orthodoxy,
             You and your valued sense
                 of self,
             You and whatever you bring
                 with you, for self-serving,
                         for self-sufficiency.
We stand addressed,
    invited to travel light without encumberment,
                 the things we treasure and carry
                 along without notice.

In this season of new life and dazzling new beginning,
Grant that we begin again, addressed,
> responsive,
> not "swept away" by
> your impatience.

Give us freedom to travel light before you this day,
> just us without defining
> accoutrement.

We pray in the name of the One
who traveled light, with
> no purse,
> no bag,
> no sandals (Luke 10:4),
> free and powerful,
> alive and enlivening,
> even Jesus. Amen.

—April 4, 2002, Columbia Theological Seminary

Great God of power and sovereignty,
Strong God of governance and order,
Decisive God of the rising and falling
of all worldly power:
    We ponder the drastic ways in which
        you allow worldly power to surge;
    We notice the horizon of mercy by which
        you measure power;
    We watch while you put the other gods to flight,
        and end in your self-assertive doxology.
In the end, we are glad that it is you,
              who gives power, and
              who curbs power.
    We rest easier in your governance,
        and then . . . as we finish and end in assurance,
                out of the corner of our eye,
                   at the edge of the text,
We notice that it is our power as superpower
that is curbed,
           it is our menacing that is judged by
              your mercy,
           it is our self-sufficiency that is
              drawn short by your plentitude.
As always with you, we are jarred and kept off balance,
Able only to yield power to you, Great God,
              Strong God,
              Decisive God,
    even our God, our hope and our limit. Amen.

—November 27, 2001, Columbia Theological Seminary

(On Reading Psalm 130)

A thousand ages in your sight are like an evening gone.
  You, Lord of all creation, seem to work in slow time.
  In your slow time you formed the world
      and all that is in it.
  At your slow pace, you called into life the plants,
      animals, and sea creatures.
  In your slow readiness, you sit present
      to the aches of the world.
  In your slow pause you bring the world
      to newness in ways we do not comprehend.
And we, your faithful people,
      Mostly live in fast time.
  Life is short for us, and we want it full;
  Life is uncertain for us, and we want to know;
  Life is dangerous for us,
      and we want to bring it under control.
          We want our aches healed;
          We want our doubts assuaged;
          We want our shame relieved;
          We want our hopes fulfilled.
And you meander toward us and with us,
      and beyond us,
  As though you had more time than money,
  As though you had Sabbath leave
      in the midst of our hurry.

In this moment of our haste and your slowness,
>   We ask that you reset the clock of our anxiety
>   to conform to your pace;
>   We ask that you recalibrate our hopes according
>   to your good governance;
>   We ask that you resituate our eagerness
>   into your patience.
So we pray, in your time and at your pace,
>   Make all things new;
>   Make all things new among the warring
>   tribes and nations;
>   Make all things new in our troubled economy
>   of the rich and poor,
>   the employed and the unemployed;
>   Make all things new amid our sickness, hurt, loss,
>   and despair.
We dare say, hurry, good Lord!
>   Hurry to heal the sick whom we name . . .
>   Hurry to turn our weeping into laughter;
>   Hurry to turn our enemies into neighbors;
>   Hurry, good Lord,
>   And we will praise you all day long
>   and well into the night . . .

—June 7, 2015

For the curious ways in which you keep your promises,
   we are grateful.

We are a part of your people
   who this day yearn for a safe place.
   We grudgingly hear the cries of your people
     who have less of place than do we.
   We are mindful this day of the troubled peoples
     of Lebanon, Ireland, and Rhodesia,
   and those in our own country
     who cry out for place.

Some of us have more place than we need,
   and we think we own it.

We confess to you, in the wake of Jesus Christ,
   that we are pilgrims and sojourners
     who do not own our land.

   We thank you for granting it to us for a season
     and for brothers and sisters to dwell there with us.

We pray that you hear the cries of the displaced,
   the cries of brothers and sisters,
   that you help us to see the ways in which
     our own cries are too often phony. Amen.

—September 29, 1976

Spirit of God —
  who forms and re-forms your church,
    who creates and who re-creates
      your grateful people for yourself —
We pray this day
  for a mighty rush of your Spirit;
    that the church among us
      may be re-formed and re-created.
We pray for the coming of your Spirit
  upon our brothers and sisters in Chicago,
    for the coming of your incredible Spirit
      among us all,
That out of our formlessness
  we may be re-formed,
    and out of our chaos
      we may be re-created.

We know that we are creatures of your breath
  and we wait for your breathing.

We are creatures of your word
  and we wait for your speaking.

We pray for enough peace
   and enough courage and enough patience,
   that we may pause in our much-speaking
      to each other
      and wait for your speech;
   that we may leave off breathing
      on each other
      and wait for your life-giving breath.

We do not know how a church
   could be shaped after the body of Jesus,
      but you have promised it to us,
         and so we ask for new beginnings.
Amen.

—December 3, 1976

You are the God who gathers the scattered into your
well-being. We pray to you because we are
among the scattered:

> scattered in fear,
> scattered in anger,
> scattered in indifference.

We are weary of such isolation, and we yearn to be
together in one good company. Give us the freedom
and courage to forgo our fear, anger, and indifference,
that we may be joined together in the way you intend
in well-being, trust, and praise. We pray in the name
of Jesus, the one who gathers the blind, the lame, the
deaf, lepers, and the poor into one family. Amen.

—December 18, 2017

THE GOD WHO
PLUCKS UP AND TEARS DOWN

You have yet the whole world in your hands . . .
             That we do not doubt.
You are saturated with mercy, compassion,
             goodness, and generosity . . .
                  That we do not doubt.
We are—nonetheless—haunted by the witness
that you are a God with a ferocious will
who will not be mocked.
We are vexed by the awareness that
when you are mocked,
    you pluck up and tear down.
So we ponder about your ferocious will,
                  your being mocked, and
                  your plucking up and
                  tearing down.
We wonder in what ways we have mocked you,
    and in what ways you do your ferocious work.
We watch and wonder if you pluck up . . .
    We notice ways our world is being plucked up
        by the roots . . .
        Our institutions on which we have relied,
        Our certitudes that no longer seem to hold,
        Our entitlements that we cannot any longer
            protect,
        Our growth economy that we cannot any longer
            cause to grow.

We wonder and watch if you tear down . . .
　　We notice ways in which there is a tearing down
　　　　　　　among us,
　　　　Our security systems,
　　　　Our social infrastructure that makes life livable,
　　　　Our steadiness and solidity in church
　　　　　For which we can hardly pay any more.
Then we remember that, in ancient days,
　　You plucked up your people out of the land,
　　You tore down your messiah on that dread Friday,
　　You put your people into free fall,
　　　　More than twice, more than many times,
　　　　With brutality and fear and greed and
　　　　　anti-neighborliness and injustice.
We are vexed and haunted by what we know of you,
and so we pause,
　　　　To think about old texts,
　　　　To think about present circumstance.
We ask you to pluck up our systems
of greed and anxiety,
　　　　to tear down old walls of fear and exclusion,
　　　　to begin anew, filled with Easter dance.
We find ourselves on that Saturday
of plucking up and tearing down.
We notice and we wonder,
and if it is not too soon, we hope. Amen.

　　　　　　—*October 16, 2013, Columbia Theological Seminary,*
　　　　　　　　　　St. Timothy Episcopal Church

You are the lion who roars,
      and we tremble;
you are the one who sends,
      and we go;
you are the one who speaks,
      and we echo your words.

Except . . . there is such a cacophony of words . . .
      too much techno-speech,
      too much psychobabble,
      too much mindless prattle,
      too many thoughtless emails,
      too many mixed messages
        floating around in our bodies.

Even, we confess, too many of our own words
  grounded only in our fears or
            in our hopes or
            in our good intentions.

We are glad for your call to us
  and for your gift of words to us.

We ask for courage not to flinch,
      for patience to listen well,
      for wisdom to discern,
      for words that speak faithfully
        of your Friday anguish
        and of your Sunday newness.

We are among the many talkers
   who want to be summoned and addressed.
Give us fresh, thick words
   that may lead us to the Fleshed One
            wherein lies our hope and our future.

Roar, speak, send . . . here we are. Amen.

        —*January 11, 2008, Columbia Theological Seminary*
                              DMin Class

WHOSE ABUNDANCE
WE DO NOT TRUST

You are the God of good generosity;
You are the God who has commanded fruitfulness,
    blessing, and abundance in the earth;
You are the God who has ordained teeming
        oceans and populated forests and
                amber waves of grain;
You are the God of more than enough!

    And we . . .

We in our fearful anxiety,
            fear running out and
            lacking and
            having deficiency.

We in our scarcity,
            oppress and seize and grasp
            and manipulate and confiscate . . .
    because of our deficits in
                love and mercy,
                in oil and uranium,
                in grace and truth,
                in bread and wine.

    We, in our lack, doubt you and make a world of
        grudge and violence.

We ponder that incredible mismatch
     between *your goodness*
     and *our fearfulness*.
  And ask that you,
      by your life-giving spirit,
     blow our fear toward your abundance,
     that we may ease up and trust
      and bask in abundance.

You are indeed our shepherd . . . and
        we lack nothing. Amen.

—July 23, 2007, Columbia Theological Seminary
Continuing Education Event

You address us in summons,
    and our world is changed.

Your address to us is not often as clear as a letter;
    it comes to us by the move of your spirit,
                by the shatter of events,
                by the gesture of a companion,
                by a stir in the night.

And then as clear as any direct correspondence:

• You assert that we should get accustomed
        to our status of displacement
            and disorientation —
    And we dream of a return to normalcy.
    We imagine a peaceable church,
                a sound dollar,
                a compassionate society,
                an anxious-free ministry.
    And you respond, get used to the abnormal
                which is the venue of your life.

• You assert that we should get on with
    the construction of a new society;
    and we wallow in our nightmares
        of exhaustion and resentment,
        inclined to self-pity,
        self-preoccupied, waiting to be cared for.

And you respond that this
    time is for building and planting,
    time to get our minds off ourselves.

• You assert that our energy should go to the
    well-being of the city and of the empire;
    And we withdraw before issues
    that are too complex, or
    we despise the empire and secretly hope
        for its failure, or
    we wonder which city to pray for,
        D.C. or Louisville or Baghdad
        or our hometown, and in our wonderment
        in fact pray very little.
And you respond that it is time now
    to put faith toward the world crisis in the
    assurance that our faith matters
    to the coming humanity that you will.

We are mindful
> of the whispers of liberty
> that are abroad in the land,
> because you are God.

We are mindful
> of our mothers and our fathers who,
> for many generations,
> have lived variously in hope and in oppression.

We do not doubt
> that in your heart of hearts,
> freedom is what you will for all your people.

And so we thank you
> for the breakthrough of freedom
> as it is happening in our world.

We are mindful this day
> of our brothers and sisters in many places,
> in this land and in many lands,
> where the pressures of oppression
> are heavy and hopeless.

We do not understand the incongruity
> between your will for freedom
> and the reality of oppression among us.
> We do know that we stand on both sides
> and we are oppressed and we are oppressors.

And so we thank you
for your voice of freedom
and the whispers of liberty
that you have placed among us
in Jesus of Nazareth.

Amen.

—September 22, 1976

(On Reading Isaiah 56:3–8)

It seems right and good to be God's chosen people.
   We enjoyed friendship with God;
   we were assured special blessings from God;
   best of all we got the land of promise
   as our very own.
But then, immediately,
other peoples began to crowd in on us.
   First it was the Canaanites and the Philistines;
   then it was the "yellow threat" from Asia;
   later it was all the intruders from south of the border,
     and now we have to contend with too many Blacks,
     and many insistent Native Americans
       who will not go away.
       And now it is Muslims!
It has turned out that all these "others" are now with us;
   they crowd us and disturb us and compete with us.
Of necessity we devised rules to protect our specialness;
   we formulated laws of purity
   and made a list of all those things
     that disqualified others.
     We made rules for
       race and ethnicity and gender and pedigree;
     we made it all safe and secure from all alarms.

And then, right then, abruptly,
you uttered your shattering word:
    It is for "all peoples" . . .
             "my house a house of prayer"!
We blinked, we wondered, we debated:
    Did you say "all peoples"?
             All peoples like foreigners?
             All peoples like eunuchs?
             All peoples like Mexicans?
             All peoples like Muslims?
We checked the text; we interrogated the ancient poet.
    We investigated your own ancient history
        of xenophobia.
        And the word was confirmed: you did say
           "all peoples"!
In that utterance you undid our sense of specialness;
    you undermined our purity laws
        and our best self-serving formulations.
    We looked and discovered, as we had not seen,
        the sweep and wonder of your governance,
        the largeness of your vision,
        and the expansiveness of your house of prayer.
We looked and then noticed, as for the first time,
that the company of those who trust you
    is very large, very mixed, very diverse.
We watched and saw that you are gathering others
        alongside us.
    You have gathered us as your chosen,
    but your gathering does not stop with us;
        you gather others as your people.

All of us, those who have long been chosen,
   and others now gathered,
   all of us at prayer in your house;
   all of us at Sabbath in your creation;
   all of us together in covenant;
   all of us together, according to your wide purpose.
   Amen.

(On Reading Exodus 20:1–6)

The demanding, relentless brick quotas
    kept arriving at daybreak for our ancient
      mothers and fathers.
They faced the harshness of harassment;
  the heat of the kilns,
    the bristles of straw collected.
And then, abruptly, all of that ended . . .
    because you, Lord of liberty and justice,
      in an instant on a dark night,
    you led our mothers and fathers out of bondage
      in singing, in dancing, and in joy.
We remember that ancient bondage.
We recall the flash of your emancipation.

We know that bondage now among us:
      bondage of our caves
        of self-preoccupied, insular living,
      bondage of our tribes
        of the like-minded
        in fear of all others;
      bondage of the market
        and our mad chase after more;
      bondage of theater
        where we live make-believe lives.

But we ourselves also know the flash
of your emancipation. And because of that flash,
　　　　　we know who you are;
　　　　　we know the future
　　　　　　you would give us;
　　　　　we know your passion for justice;
　　　　　we know your deep love
　　　　　　for us and for our world.

And so we love you back, wholly,
without compromise or distraction,
　　　　　with all our heart,
　　　　　all our mind,
　　　　　and all our soul.
We will not so passionately love any other,
　because you are the source
　　of our life and our future.
We give you praise for your ancient deliverances.
We give you thanks for your liberating presence
　　with us now.
We give you honor and glory for your good future
　　to which you summon us.
You are the one who makes us "free at last."
　　And we love you! Amen.

We spend our time the way we do here together,
    because we do not doubt
   that your word is a lamp unto our feet
   and a light unto our path

       or

Should we pray on this post-day:
   The kings of the earth set themselves
     and the rulers take counsel together
        against the Lord . . .
   He who sits in the heavens laughs.

We have our heads turned by votes and elections
   and winners and power and arms and
   money and leverage . . .

And then we are sobered by your word
       as lamp and light.
   We are reminded of the scroll that addresses,
    the scroll that gives us place,
        that gives us memory,
        that gives us futures,
        that gives us mandates.

We know ourselves mandated by the scroll,
    to practice reconciliation,
    to stand boldly against evil,
    to trust daily bread,
    to give, to forgive, and to be forgiven.

Move your Spirit through the scroll . . .
    and through us . . .
        that we may be formed to newness
                in freedom and
                in joy.
    The freedom and newness glimpsed in the scroll
                                    fleshly enacted.
                                        Amen.

—November 3, 2004 (the morning after the U.S. election),
Columbia Theological Seminary

(DMin Day 7)

We regularly say:
  "We proclaim the Lord's death until he come."
In our primitiveness, we do not doubt your coming,
    soon, powerfully, decisively.
In our settledness, your coming is not too urgent or real,
    because we are variously entitled, privileged,
        protected, gated.
In our rationality, the "until" of your coming makes
        little sense to us,
    so we mumble and hope no one notices.
In these last days,
In these latter days,
In these final days,
In these very late days,
    We draw closer to your promised "until."
    We draw closer in fear,
                    in hope,
                    in gladness,
                    in dread.
So we do proclaim the Lord's death until he come,
    until he come in peace against all our violence;
    until he come in generosity midst all our parsimony;
    until he come in food midst all our hunger;
    until he come in community midst all our alienation.

We are your faithful hopers,
   distracted by despair, but hoping,
   distracted by affluence, but hoping;
   distracted by sophistication, but hoping.
Come soon, come, Lord Jesus, come soon
   while we face afresh your death,
   until you come soon and again . . . again and soon.
      Amen.

   —*October 30, 2001, Columbia Theological Seminary*

(First Sunday in Lent)

We boldly address you as creator of heaven and earth.
But we come into your presence
- inundated by the destructive reverberations
of Katrina
and all those disasters we call "natural."
- overwhelmed by the inhumane threats of war
and terror and brutality . . .
and the world feels to us unglued,
and we are fearful.

And then caught up short by your "never again,"
never again floodwaters to overwhelm,
never again barbarism we cannot bear,
never again threats to our life and
our sense of coherence.

We boldly address you as Lord of our life,
but we enter into your presence
- having divided the world up into good and bad,
friend and foe, us and them,
- divided up in fear and resistance and even hate
when they threaten *us* and place us . . .
so it seems . . . in jeopardy.

But we are caught up short by your "all flesh":
	all flesh in your mercy and fidelity,
	all flesh like snakes and scorpions,
	all flesh like our families with whom we are askew,
	all flesh like our neighbor who irritates us,
	all flesh like Muslims who dress funny,
	all flesh like immigrants who move in next to us,
	all flesh like gays so unlike us,
			except that they are our precious children,
	You love all flesh, and we are linked to them
		in your mercy.

We boldly address you as our faithful savior.
	But we come into your presence
		sensing that we are forgotten
			even if not left behind,
		ignored, disregarded, trivialized, unappreciated . . .

And then we are caught up short
by your rainbow remembrance,
	the light of glory that shines
			through waters of generosity,
		light and water made into rainbow reminder,
	and we sense that we are more remembered and
		taken seriously than we had noticed.

We rally to your word:
				Never again,
				all flesh,
				rainbow remembered.

We are shaken out of our mistaken self-perception
and drawn to you.
You are our home, our maker, our lover, our hope . . .
And we are yours! Amen.

—March 5, 2006